Nestlé Smarties ®

PIRATES

D0528313

Other Smarties titles available:

Smarties Beautiful Beasties
Smarties Book of Wizardry
Smarties Chuckle Factory
Smarties Deadly Dinosaurs
Smarties Dinosaur Jokes
Smarties Hairy Humans
Smarties Hilariously Funny Verse
Smarties How To Draw Cartoons
Smarties How To Make 'em Laugh Joke Book
Smarties How To Be Really Smart Joke Book
Smarties Knock Knock Joke Book
Smarties Practical Jokes
Smarties Puzzle Busters
Smarties Smart Science
Smarties Travel Teasers
Smarties Wacky World
Smarties Wizard Jokes

SMARTIES® PIRATES

By Justin Scroggie

Illustrations by DAVID MOSTYN

Robinson Children's Books

First published in the UK by Robinson Children's Books,
an imprint of Constable & Robinson Ltd, 2002

Constable & Robinson Ltd
3 The Lanchesters
162 Fulham Palace Road
London W6 9ER
www.constablerobinson.com

Text © Justin Scroggie 2002
Illustrations © David Mostyn 2002

NESTLÉ and SMARTIES are registered trademarks of Société des
Produits Nestlé S.A., 1800 Vevey, Switzerland.
© 2002 Société des Produits Nestlé S.A., Vevey, Switzerland.
Trade Mark Owners

All rights reserved. This book is sold subject to the condition that it
shall not, by way of trade or otherwise, be lent, re-sold, hired out or
otherwise circulated in any form of binding or cover other than that
in which it is published and without a similar condition including this
condition being imposed on the subsequent purchaser.

A copy of the British Library Cataloguing in Publication Data for
this title is available from the British Library.

ISBN 1-84119-548-0

Printed and bound in the EU
Nørhaven Paperback, Denmark
10 9 8 7 6 5 4 3 2 1

Introduction

Yo! Ho! Ho!

*Do you know why pirates wear gold earrings?
How Blackbeard made his hair smoke?
Which disease pirates got from parrot poo?*

Young Jake is struggling with his school project on 'Pirates', when he rubs an old gold coin his dad found in a junk shop ...

Amazingly he conjures up an eighteenth-century buccaneer pirate, Cap'n Blackbird – eyepatch, parrot and all! The Cap'n takes Jake aboard his pirate ship, *The Leaky Bucket,* and shows him what life was *really* like for PIRATES!

Find out what pirates ate (yuk!), how much they drank (lots!), what they wore (oh dear), how they fought (dirtily), how they lived (wow!) and how they died (horribly)!

Introduction

GASP at the stories of the legendary Captain Kidd, Henry Morgan and Black Bart. SHUDDER at the secrets of the black flag, including the 'Jolly Roger'. BE SHOCKED at the rules by which pirates lived, and TREMBLE at the terrible punishments suffered by those who disobeyed them ...

At the end of the book you'll find a treasure map. If you've read the book you'll be able to solve the clues and find out where the treasure is buried!

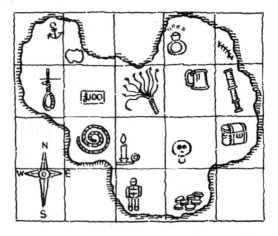

So stir your stumps, shiver your timbers and set sail with Jake, Blackbird, his pirate parrot Harriet and the motley crew of *The Leaky Bucket* as they roam the Seven Seas, searching for TREASURE ...

Jake

Jake's school project on PIRATES is not going well . . .

Jake

For the project Jake's dad had bought him an old Spanish coin called a 'doubloon' . . .

Captain Blackbird

Captain Blackbird

Beardless Bob

There's a tremendous **FLASH!** and Jake finds himself on the deck of *The Leaky Bucket!*

*'Grommet' is the pirate word for 'cabin boy'

Grubber & Q

*In charge of stores including weapons

Advert

Enterprising, adventurous, water–based company seeks

CABIN BOY

Duties include fetching, carrying, swabbing, sweeping, cleaning, climbing, light slavery. Also some fighting.

We offer seven-year contract, all food and board, plus great opportunities for travel. Candidate must have clean sailing licence, head for heights, strong stomach, own uniform and head lice.

All enquiries c/o Molly's Tavern, Stowaway Lane, Portsmouth

Greek Pirates

One pirate complained to Alexander the Great:

*The word 'piracy' comes from the ancient Greek word for attack.

Romans & Vikings

Roman pirates kidnapped young Julius Caesar for five weeks. They released him after a ransom was paid. Then Julius returned and killed them.

*The word 'Viking' means 'going on a raid overseas'!

Medieval Pirates

People thought 13th-century pirate Eustace the Monk used magic to make his ship invisible. Didn't stop him losing his head!

Crow's-nest

Jake joins the crew and asks Cap'n Blackbird where he should go first.

Rigging Maze

That night Jake dreams about a RAT trapped in the rigging. Can you help it find the way down to the CHEESE on the deck?

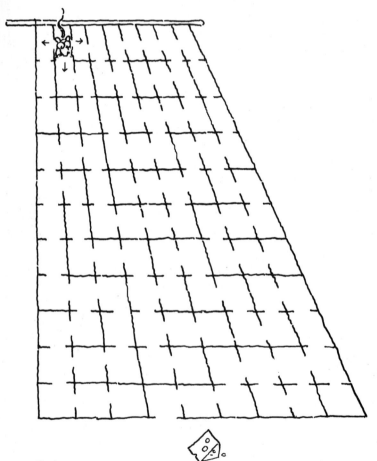

Answer on page 156

The Golden Age

The next day Jake asked Beardless Bob
more about pirates ...

Corsairs

Corsairs

Privateers

*Short for 'private men-of-war'.

Privateers

LETTER OF MARQUE
Know ye that we have
granted and given license
to _____
to annoy our enemies at
sea or by land . . . so that
they shall share with us
half their gain.

Letters like these gave privateers like **Walter Raleigh** and **Francis Drake** permission to attack Spanish ships. French privateers attacked so many English ships that King Louis 14th tried to borrow money from them!

Francis Drake

ENGLISH HERO?

To the English, Drake was a hero who attacked the hated Spanish…

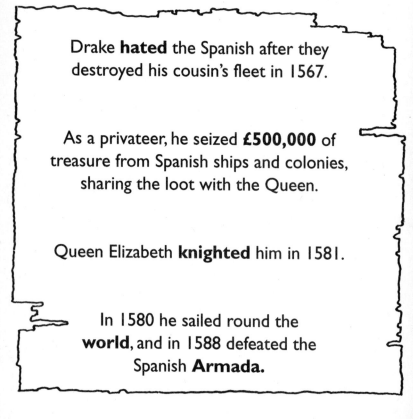

Drake **hated** the Spanish after they destroyed his cousin's fleet in 1567.

As a privateer, he seized **£500,000** of treasure from Spanish ships and colonies, sharing the loot with the Queen.

Queen Elizabeth **knighted** him in 1581.

In 1580 he sailed round the **world**, and in 1588 defeated the Spanish **Armada.**

Francis Drake

or WICKED PIRATE?

To the Spanish, Drake was a pirate who would steal anything...

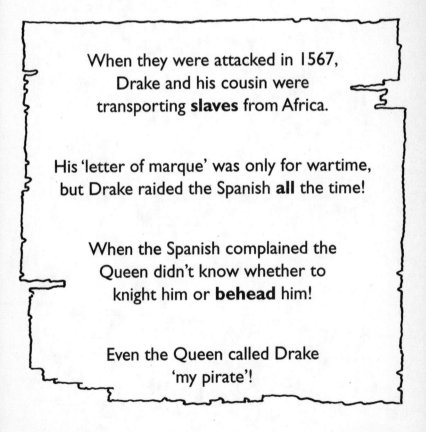

When they were attacked in 1567, Drake and his cousin were transporting **slaves** from Africa.

His 'letter of marque' was only for wartime, but Drake raided the Spanish **all** the time!

When the Spanish complained the Queen didn't know whether to knight him or **behead** him!

Even the Queen called Drake 'my pirate'!

Buccaneers

AFTER THE PRIVATEERS CAME THE BUCCANEERS!

In 1603 King James cancelled all 'Letters of Marque'.

Many British, French and Dutch privateers became **pirates** instead!

YE PIRATE'S

WHY CALL THEMSELVES BUCCANEERS?

AFTER CARIBBEAN ISLANDERS WHO SMOKED ANIMAL SKINS IN OVENS CALLED 'BOUCANS'

VERY SMELLY

Buccaneers

The Spanish attacked these 'boucaniers', so they raided Spanish treasure ships . . .

'BOUCANIERS' = BUCCANEERS! I GET IT!

THE BUCCANEERS WERE JOINED BY CONVICTS, SLAVES, EX-SOLDIERS - ANYONE AFTER TREASURE.

BURIED TREASURE

Later they raided merchant ships trading with the Far East...

Buccaneer Search

Can you find five buccaneers – KIDD, BART, MORGAN, AVERY and TEACH – hidden in these islands? Their names are written forwards or backwards, up or down, right to left, or diagonally.

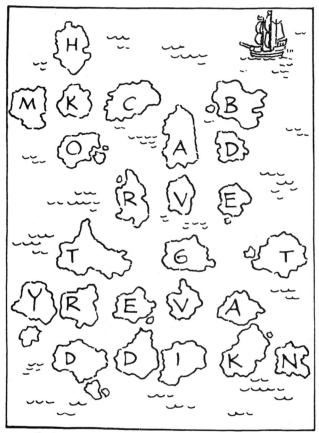

Answer on page 156

Make Cap'n Blackbird's Hat

1. Put two pieces of black card *together* and cut out this shape:

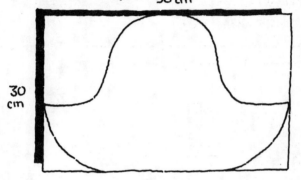

50 cm

30 cm

2. Cut out a skull and two bones:

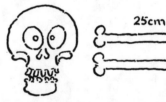

25cm

3. Stick the skull and crossbones on to the hat and staple* the ends **together**:

*Ask an adult to help you to be safe.

The Leaky Bucket

Jake wanted to find out more about *The Leaky Bucket* . . .

The Leaky Bucket

AHOY!

Captain Blackbird of The Leaky Bucket welcomes AHOY! *Magazine to his luxury floating home!*

Blackbird in his cabin at the rear ('stern'). 'It's my special place,' says the Cap'n. 'There's not much privacy aboard!'

'Grommet' Jake relaxes in the crow's-nest (or 'foretop') high above the deck, looking for ships, land or storms.

The Leaky Bucket

Quartermaster Desmond shows off one of the ship's 46 cannons. Each ball weighs 5 kg!

The Leaky Bucket is 35 metres long from bow to stern, weighs 260 tonnes, and has a crew of 151 sailors and a top speed of 25 km/h!

Safety is top priority in the gunpowder room. First mate Bob shows us why candles, pistols and smoking are forbidden here!

The Leaky Bucket

When the ship leaves port, happy pirates gather round the capstan for a singsong – oh, and they raise the anchor too!

At the bow (front) is this figurehead: 'a tribute to my mother' says Blackbird. It's also a handy battering ram!

Next week in **AHOY!** *. . . an interview with piratess Ann Bonny ('I love being a single mum!') and full coverage of Calico Jack's hanging.*

Treasure: The Spanish Main

TELL ME ABOUT TREASURE!

IN THE 1500s, SPAIN INVADED CENTRAL AND SOUTH AMERICA...THEY SEIZED GOLD, SILVER AND JEWELLERY FROM THE TEMPLES.

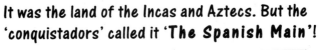

It was the land of the Incas and Aztecs. But the 'conquistadors' called it '**The Spanish Main**'!

Treasure: The Spanish Main

Precious metal was melted into **blocks** for shipping . . .

...or gold coins called 'doubloons' ...

...or silver coins called 'pieces-of-eight'.*

For 150 years the treasure was shipped to Spain in huge galleons, crewed by 200 men in massive convoys . . .

*This was because they were worth 8 'reals'.

Treasure: The Spanish Main

Pirates attacked treasure galleons early in their voyages. Ships couldn't go fast till they found a strong wind to power the sails.

Treasure: Great Trade Routes

IN THE 17ᵀᴴ CENTURY, EUROPE BEGAN TO TRADE GOODS WITH COUNTRIES LIKE INDIA AND CHINA...

ENGLAND

THE GREAT TRADE ROUTES

CHINA

INDIA

AFRICA

INDIAN OCEAN

MADAGASCAR

CAPE OF GOOD HOPE

MERCHANT SHIPS CALLED 'EAST INDIAMEN' SAILED THE GREAT 'TRADE ROUTES'- AND SO DID THE PIRATES!

Treasure: Great Trade Routes

SHIPS CARRIED GOLD AND SILVER TO TRADE FOR:

SILK, IVORY, LEATHER, FURS . . .

SPICES LIKE NUTMEG AND CINNAMON . . .

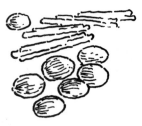

SUGAR, TEA, COFFEE, COCOA BEANS . . .

CHINA, SALT, TOBACCO . . .

Thomas Tew

In 1693, pirate Thomas Tew attacked a merchant ship returning to Bombay and seized loot worth over £3,000 to each crew member.

Treasure

PIRATES ALSO STOLE CHARTS, COMPASSES, TELESCOPES, FLAGS, SAILS...

When Black Bart seized the *King Solomon* he chucked all the cargo overboard –except for the **ropes** ...!

TO LAWLESS PIRATES, MEDICINE CHESTS WERE REAL TREASURE!

Treasure Chest Of Jokes

Did you hear about the pirate
who only stole coins?

He thought the change would
do him good!

What is a pirate's favourite
musical instrument?

The lute!

What do pirates eat?

Pieces of ate!

Joining Up

Cap'n Blackbird's **SIX** reasons to become a pirate!

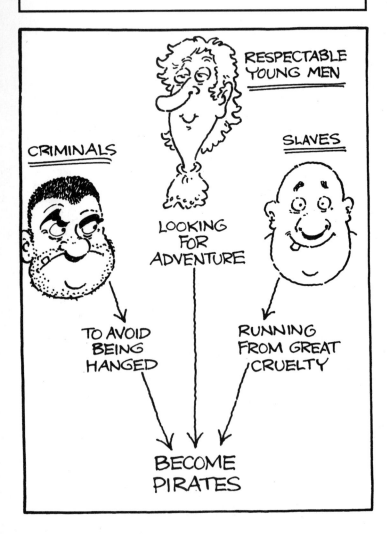

RESPECTABLE YOUNG MEN

CRIMINALS

SLAVES

LOOKING FOR ADVENTURE

TO AVOID BEING HANGED

RUNNING FROM GREAT CRUELTY

BECOME PIRATES

Joining Up

Cap'n Blackbird's **SIX** reasons to become a pirate!

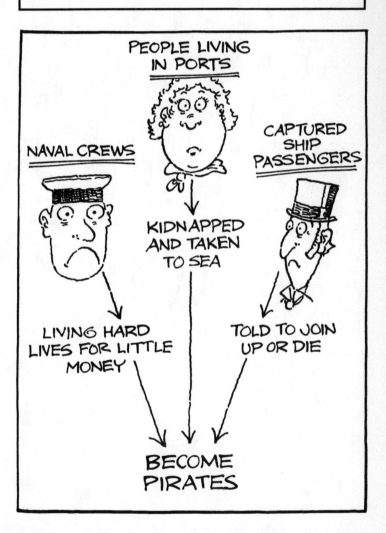

PEOPLE LIVING IN PORTS

NAVAL CREWS

CAPTURED SHIP PASSENGERS

KIDNAPPED AND TAKEN TO SEA

LIVING HARD LIVES FOR LITTLE MONEY

TOLD TO JOIN UP OR DIE

BECOME PIRATES

Ships

Sloops

Brigantines

Junks

OR EVEN A JUNK LIKE MADAME CHENG'S...

4 SQUARE SAILS STRETCHED ON BAMBOO *

SHALLOW HULL

VERY LIGHT, SO FAST AND EASY TO TURN

*Though this is easily destroyed by fire!

Ships

Brigantine Of Jokes!

What did one side of the pirate
ship say to the other?

I'll meet you round the front!

What does every pirate ship weigh?

Its anchor!

When is a pirate ship like snow?

When it's adrift!

Which pirate ship sits at the
bottom of the sea and shakes?

A nervous wreck!

Captain Blackbird's Guide to Fighting

1. Creep up on your victims when they are asleep.

2. Raise a friendly flag you've stolen.

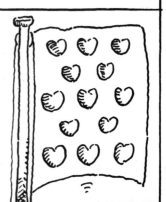

3. Hide your crew or dress 'em up as women passengers . . .

4. At the last moment, run up the Jolly Roger – pirates ahoy!

Captain Blackbird's Guide to Fighting

5. Tell 'em to surrender, or expect no mercy.

SURRENDER!

6. Shout bloodthirsty curses, beat drums, blow horns and fire pistols!

7. Fire cannons high to trash the mast.

8. Use grappling irons to pull the ship close.

Captain Blackbird's Guide to Fighting

9. Climb up the sides with axes – it's time to fight hand-to-hand.

10. Invite their crew to join you or be set adrift.

11. Tell passengers to hand over valuables.

12. If it's a nice ship, scuttle yours and rename the new one . . . job done!

Compensation

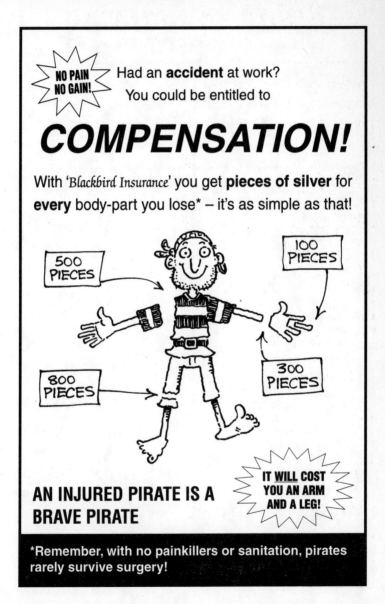

Most Wanted

Most Wanted

CHARLOTTE DE BERRY

RAHMAH BIN JABR

SHE AND HER CREW ATE 2 SLAVES—AND HER HUSBAND

BLEW UP HIS OWN SHIP TO DESTROY ENEMY FLEET.

Pirates' Victims

Chinese pirates kept their prisoners in bamboo cages.

Some prisoners were used for target practice, running round the deck being shot at.

Some were used as 'horses', racing round the ship!

Really unlucky victims were cooked, stretched with ropes or eaten alive by cockroaches!

Walking the Plank

Walking the Plank

Mind the Sharks!

Jake has to swim from the plank to the shore without meeting a shark. Can you show him the way?

Answer on page 157

Women Pirates

In the eighteenth century, life for women could be very boring, so many dressed up as men to join the army or go to sea ...

*In case the men fought each *other*, not the enemy!

Princess Alwida

ALWIDA was a Goth princess from Sweden about 1,500 years ago ...

Alwida and her all-women crew terrorized the Baltic until Alf fought bravely to get her back!

Mary Read & Ann Bonny

Mary was raised as a boy and joined the army disguised as a man.

When pirate Calico Jack seized her ship in the Caribbean, Mary joined the crew.

SURPRISE!

Aboard she met Ann Bonny (also dressed as a man!) whom she fancied, until . . .

Mary, Ann and Jack raided Spanish treasure ships till the British Navy caught them.

SURPRISE!

SURPRISE!

Mary Read & Ann Bonny

Only Mary and Ann fought – the rest of the crew were drunk and scared.

Before Jack was hanged, Ann told him:

HAD YOU FOUGHT LIKE A MAN, YOU NEEDN'T HAVE BEEN HANGED LIKE A DOG.

Ann and Mary weren't hanged, because they were both pregnant.

SURPRISE!

Mary died of Yellow Fever, but Ann was bought out of jail by her rich dad.

SURPRISE!

Madame Cheng

Madame Cheng was the widow of a Chinese pirate.

Her husband left Cheng his huge 'Red Flag' fleet. She and her number two, Chang Pao, raided Chinese ships and ports for 3 years.

In 1810 the government offered her a pardon if she gave up piracy.

Cheng opened a gambling house and died old and rich!

The Cutlass

When Jake asked the Quartermaster what kind of weapons pirates used for fighting, Desmond brandished a nasty-looking cutlass!*

*Based on butchers' knives used by early buccaneers!

The Musket

Next minute he was looking down the barrel of a musket!

*Jolly difficult on a rolling deck!

The Pistol

Desmond had some handy advice about pistols!

*Pirates used axes to climb the steep sides of an enemy ship!

The Cannon

Then it was on to the gun-deck for a look at the cannons.

*Balls were called 'shot'; iron bits were 'grapeshot'!

Explosive Facts!

Gunpowder is a mixture of saltpetre, sulphur and charcoal.

It was invented by the Chinese around AD 800: Arabs called it 'Chinese snow'.

By the sixteenth century, gun-barrels were strong enough to use gunpowder without exploding!

Two hundred buccaneers died when the magazine on Henry Morgan's ship accidentally blew up.

Pirates filled boats with gunpowder, set them alight, and pushed them into the enemy fleet – where they blew up!

Musket Of Jokes

Do you like cannon balls?

Dunno, I've never been invited to one!

How was gunpowder invented?

In a flash!

Where do pirates fight duels?

On the duel carriageway!

How do you know when a cutlass is cross?

It looks daggers at you!

Clothes

Clothes

NEW CLOTHES COST A FORTUNE, SO PIRATES STEAL 'EM!

JIM'S GOT A HANKIE ON 'IS 'EAD AND ROUND HIS NECK...

..WOOLLY SHIRT, BELTED AT THE WAIST, TARRED TO MAKE IT WATERPROOF...

...CANVAS TROUSERS WE CALL 'SLOPPES' MADE FROM OLD SAILS...

Clothes

Make Jim's Headscarf

1. Take a square of material.

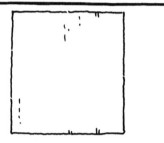

2. Fold it in half to make a triangle. Put it on your head with the longest side above your eyes.

3. Tie the two narrowest ends at the back of your head.

4. Tuck the loose wide end into the knot.

Pocketful Of Jokes

What did one pirate earring say to
the other?

Between you and me, we need a
haircut!

This collar's <u>really</u> tight.

You've put your head through a
sleeve, stupid!

Why did the pirate throw his shoes
away?

Because they were sticking their
tongues out at him!

Buried Treasure?

Buried Treasure?

Pirates' lives were too short to bury loot: they **spent** it!

Maps were unreliable – they probably couldn't find the same island **twice!**

Pirates weren't **dumb** enough to draw maps showing where their loot was!

Huge oak treasure chests bound with iron and locked were **bolted** to the deck.

A chest filled with gold coins weighed half a tonne – too **heavy** to bury or dig up!

Sharing The Loot

In the event The Leaky Bucket
captures treasure, it shall be shared as follows:

CAPTAIN – 2 Shares

SHIP'S MASTER
FIRST MATE   } – 1¹/₂ Shares
BOSUN

DOCTOR
GUNNER   } – 1¹/₄ Shares

REST OF CREW – 1 Share
CARPENTER – ³/₄ Share
(as he doesn't fight)

<u>Plus</u> pillaging (robbing passengers of their
necklaces, rings, snuff-boxes, daggers, etc.)

Life On Board

Jake is amazed how **NOISY** it is on a pirate ship.

Life On Board

With 150 unwashed sailors on board it is cramped, dark and smelly!

Life On Board

Pirates were also sailors – and a sailor's life was very **HARD WORK**!

Gambling

Mostly pirates were hanging around, waiting for someone to attack. During the boring bits, they gambled ...

The whole point of piracy was to get RICH! So it was pretty dumb to gamble away your winnings!

Cockroach Racing

1. Copy this shape and cut it out carefully.*

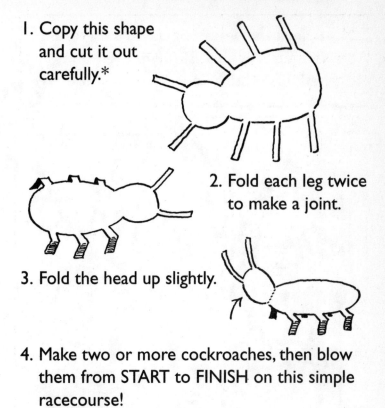

2. Fold each leg twice to make a joint.

3. Fold the head up slightly.

4. Make two or more cockroaches, then blow them from START to FINISH on this simple racecourse!

*Ask an adult to help with scissors.

Mock Trials

Most pirates expected to die by hanging. So they staged mock trials, where everyone dressed up and the Cap'n was the judge!

Music

Henry Avery

As the pirates swabbed the decks, Beardless Bob sang about a man so famous he was called the Arch-Pirate!

Tell me the tale of a pirate king
Whom folks called Henry Avery,
And 'Captain Bridgeman' <u>and</u> 'Long Ben'
- a rascal most unsavoury!

A Navy man for many years,
He became a privateer.
He forced the crew to mutiny
And became a man to fear!

He seized the ship and titled it
The Fancy — what a name!
The crew made him their captain.
(Wouldn't you have done the same?)

He put a fleet together, and
Attacked the Indian fleet.
He captured the Gang-I-Sawai,
An achievement hard to beat!

Henry Avery

Avery couldn't believe his luck!
Aboard the ship he found
A treasure trove of jewels worth
Three hundred thousand pounds!

The treasure was so huge (two grand
For each man in his crew!)
That Avery retired and fled
To start his life anew.

The English, cross with Avery, put
A bounty on his head.
They ordered Captain Kidd to bring
Him down – alive or dead!

Back to England Avery fled
Where, just as he had feared,
His crew were hanged or banished,
But old Henry . . . disappeared!

Pirate Rules

Even though they were robbers and murderers, pirates had their own rules of behaviour and swore to obey them – over an axe!

...If you sleep on watch
run away in a battle
or bring women aboard...

If you mutiny,
threaten the Cap'n
or steal more than 1 piece-of-eight...

Pirate Rules

If you hurt each other (badly!) smoke below decks, or carry an uncovered candle ...

If you keep a big secret from your shipmates ...

If you let your axe, cutlass or pistol get rusty ...

Ship's Cat or Cat O' Nine Tails

What's the Difference?

SHIP'S CAT!

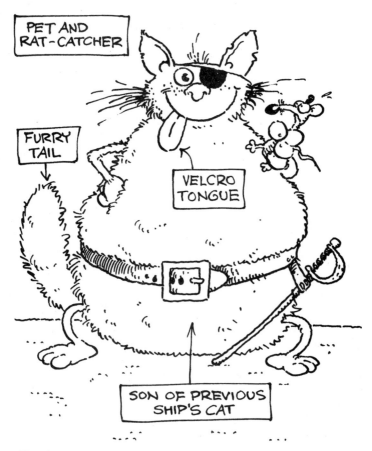

PET AND RAT-CATCHER

FURRY TAIL

VELCRO TONGUE

SON OF PREVIOUS SHIP'S CAT

Ship's Cat Or Cat O' Nine Tails

What's the Difference?

CAT O' NINE TAILS!

9 ROPY 'TAILS'

NASTY PIRATE WHIP

MADE BY PIRATE ABOUT TO BE LASHED!

KNOT ON EACH 'TAIL'

Edward England

In 1720, pirate Edward England (who was Irish!) seized the *Cassandra*, a trading ship of the East India Company.

Instead of killing the crew, he gave them his damaged pirate ship!

His own pirate crew were furious!

They set England adrift in a raft with no map. Amazingly he rowed to Madagascar, but soon died.

Marooned!

Pirates who mutinied were **marooned** on a desert island with a pistol, a water bottle, gunpowder and ammo. Without food and shelter, they soon died.

In 1704, Scottish privateer **Alexander Selkirk** argued with his captain and *asked* to be marooned!

Marooned!

With plenty of water and animals, Selkirk survived for five years. When English captain Woodes Rogers rescued him, Selkirk wanted to stay!

Rogers put Selkirk's story in his book *Cruising Voyage Round the World*. Daniel Defoe based *Robinson Crusoe* on Selkirk.

Desert Island Jokes

Which Caribbean Islands are known for their sheep?

The Baaa-hamas!

What did one dodo say to the other?

Hide – we're supposed to be extinct!

Two shipwrecked pirates:

'Do you think we're going to die?'
'Course not – here comes the Titanic!'

Drink

When Jake goes to the galley to get a cup of water, he gets a shock!

Drink

Pirates drank up to a **gallon** of alcoholic drink every day (to forget how bad their food tasted!) – no wonder they were often drunk!

Splice The Mainbrace

Every morning, Bob shouts that it's time to 'Splice the Mainbrace', and the crew get really happy!

BUT WHAT DOES IT MEAN?

IT'S SLANG FOR 'COME AND GET YOUR DAILY TOT OF RUM'

The 'mainbrace' was the rope supporting the crosspiece of a ship. To 'splice' a rope, you weaved two ends together, or fixed one end so that it didn't fray.

Toasting Game

GIVE EACH SHIPMATE A CUP OF FIZZ. EVERYONE MUST COPY THIS TOAST EXACTLY BEFORE THEY DRINK!

1. 'I drink a toast to Blackbeard, Black Bart, Ann Bonny and all buccaneers!'

2. Bow to your left. Bow to your right.

3. Repeat with both fingers in your ear.

4. Blink three times.

5. Tap your forehead with your right thumb, then your left thumb.

6. Kiss your cup, then drink – if you made no mistakes!

Food

MENU

Fried Cackle Fruit

~

Smoked Junk

~

Boiled Turtle

~

Hard Tack

~

Bumboo to drink
Tobacco (chew only)

Food

I'M ON A SEAFOOD DIET!

I SEE FOOD AND I EAT IT!

Eggs from hens on board!

Meat was salted and smoked to make it last. It was so tough pirates called it 'junk' –their name for old rope!

Turtles lived aboard till time to be eaten.

Biscuits – eaten in the dark so you couldn't see the weevils!

Rum mixed with sugar and nutmeg.

Smoking was banned because fire was a big danger on a ship.

Make Your Own Hard Tack

1. Put flour (3 cups), salt ($\frac{1}{2}$ teaspoon) and dried yeast ($\frac{1}{2}$ sachet) into a bowl.

2. Gradually add 2 big spoonfuls of water.

3. Knead into dough. Leave for 30 minutes.

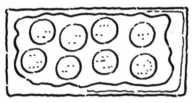

4. Roll to 1 cm thick, cut out biscuit shapes and prick with a fork.

5. Put on a baking tray. Bake on 420°F/215°C/ Gas Mark 7 for 30 minutes.*

6. Remove from oven, leave to cool and eat!

*Ask an adult for help.

Barrel Load Of Jokes

What do big strong pirates eat?

Mussels!

Did you wash that fish before you cooked it?

No! It's been in water all its life!

What do pirates call a barrel of rum?

A thirst-aid kid!

What's worse than biting into a biscuit and finding a weevil?

Finding half a weevil!

William Kidd

That night Cap'n Blackbird settled down with an old book to read about Captain Kidd.

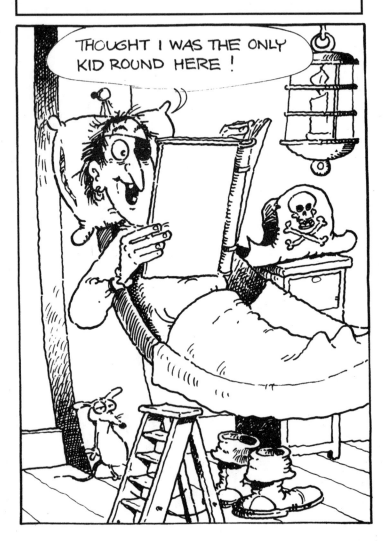

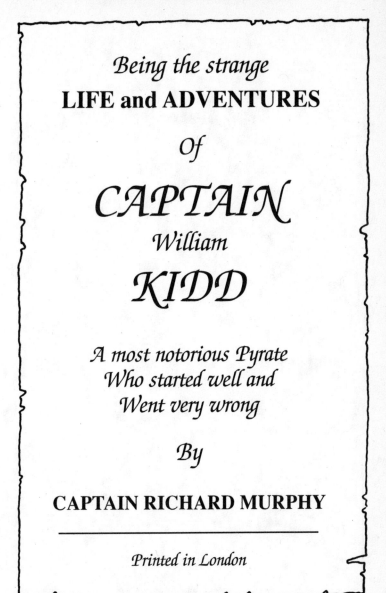

Being the strange
LIFE and ADVENTURES

Of

CAPTAIN

William

KIDD

A most notorious Pyrate
Who started well and
Went very wrong

By

CAPTAIN RICHARD MURPHY

Printed in London

William Kidd

William Kidd

*I*t is a great MYSTERY why Kidd became a pirate, for he had great fortune before.

This Scotsman was first a Privateer, chasing the hated French. Then he did become a Ship Owner of wealth, and much respected in NEW YORK.

In the Year of our Lord 1695, Captain Kidd was honoured to receive a ROYAL Commission. By strange fate he was ordered to hunt PIRATES who were plundering our merchant ships – among them the infamous Henry Avery!

Kidd built a new ship, the 'Adventure Galley', at Portsmouth, and set sail for the Indian Ocean.

William Kidd

Upon arrival, Kidd turned PIRATE. It is believed his crew threatened to MUTINY otherwise. Certainly, when the Captain did refuse to attack a Dutch ship, his crew rebelled. Kidd struck gunner William Moore on the head with a bucket and KILLED the fellow.

In the Year of our Lord 1698 Kidd did capture the Armenian ship 'Qedagh Merchant'. Legend tells that he gained plunder worth £400,000! He sent his own leaky 'Galley' to the bottom of the sea.

In the West Indies, Kidd learned he was now called 'PIRATE'. Immediately he sailed to New York to plead his INNOCENCE.

William Kidd

He left eleven bags of silver and gold on Gardiner's Island, New York.

The governor of New York did not flinch but sent Kidd to LONDON. He was held in the foulness of Newgate Prison for a whole year.

At his trial Kidd was convicted of piracy and killing Moore, and condemned to DEATH. It took two ropes to HANG Kidd: the first rope broke. His body was covered in tar and hung from a gibbet near ports or rivers as a warning to others.

The last mystery of Captain Kidd is this: Eleven bags of plunder were found on Gardiner's Island. But only the dead pirate knows where the rest of his fortune lies!

Navigation

Captains used a 'cross-staff' to work out their latitude — how far they had sailed north or south.

Later, John Harrison's 'marine chronometer' was accurate enough to work out 'longitude' — how far you to sail East or West.

Captain's Log

*Hence the word <u>logbook</u> where the captain records speed, distance and compass directions!

Knotty Facts

Later pirates threw a log off the back of the ship attached to a ROPE.

The rope had KNOTS at regular intervals.

They paid out the rope, and used an HOURGLASS to measure how long it took.

And that's where the word '**<u>knot</u>**' comes from — a measurement of SPEED at sea!

Maps

Map books (they called 'em 'waggoners') were rare, highly prized and usually stolen!

Make Your Own Pirate Map

YOU NEED:

Thick white paper
Teabag
Scissors
Pencil and crayons

PIRATE MAPS ARE REALLY FUN TO MAKE.

1. Cut the edges of the paper into wavy lines.

2. Scrunch it into a ball, then flatten it out.

3. Rub it all over with a cold wet teabag, and leave it to dry.

4. Pencil in your own pirate island, then go over in a black pen.

Make Your Own Pirate Map

5. Colour the land light green and the sea light blue.

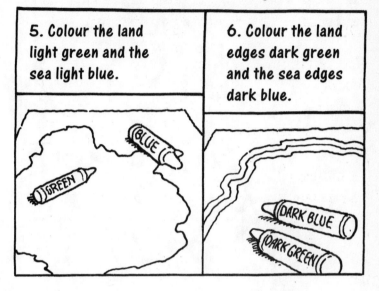

6. Colour the land edges dark green and the sea edges dark blue.

7. Add symbols: look-outs, palm trees, hills, etc.

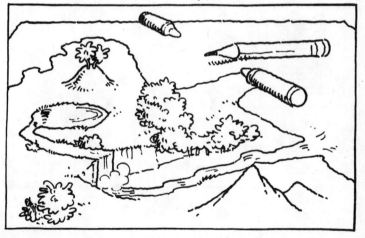

Telescopes

From the seventeenth century pirates used telescopes* to navigate, observe the weather and spot victims, like this East Indiaman ship:

*Invented in 1608 by spectacle-maker Hans Lippershey who called it a *kijker* or 'looker'.

Telescopes

Flags

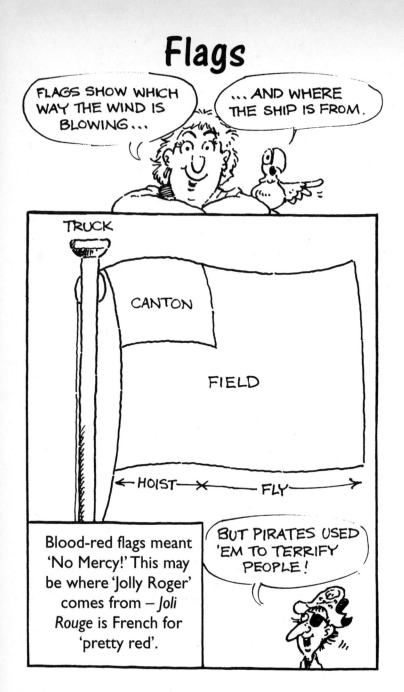

FLAGS SHOW WHICH WAY THE WIND IS BLOWING...

...AND WHERE THE SHIP IS FROM.

TRUCK

CANTON

FIELD

←—HOIST—→←—FLY—→

Blood-red flags meant 'No Mercy!' This may be where 'Jolly Roger' comes from – *Joli Rouge* is French for 'pretty red'.

BUT PIRATES USED 'EM TO TERRIFY PEOPLE!

Personal Flags

Later pirates liked BLACK flags, often with their own scary designs.

CALICO JACK RACKHAM

BLACK BART

CHRISTOPHER CONDENT

Personal Flags

THOMAS TEW

BLACKBEARD

HENRY AVERY

*Chinese pirates put bats on their flags as a sign of good luck.

Make Your Own Pirate Logo

Copy out these symbols on white paper and cut them out. Then arrange your favourites however you like on a piece of black paper.

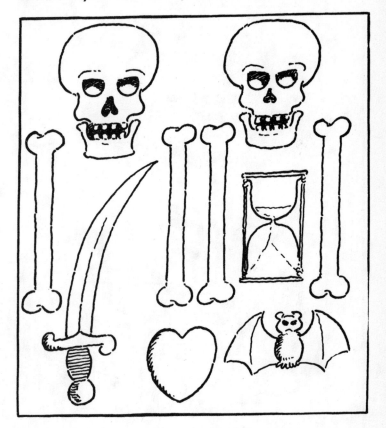

*The hourglass told victims their time was running out!

Black Bart

Jake asks Harriet if she has always been Cap'n Blackbird's parrot.

Black Bart

The slave ship Bart was working on was seized by pirates.

The pirates made Bart captain when theirs was killed in a raid.

He seized gold, jewels and tobacco from the Portuguese.

He plundered 400 ships from Africa to Newfoundland.

Black Bart

His ships included *Royal Rover, Fortune, Good Fortune* and *Royal Fortune!*

Bart drank tea, not rum, saying drunken sailors don't work well!

In 1722 he did battle with the British Navy's man-of-war *Swallow.*

Bart was shot in the neck and his crew hanged.

HE WAS A PIRATE FOR LESS THAN THREE YEARS.

Fictional Pirates Quiz

Have you seen pirates in films or read about them in books? Harriet has – and here's her quiz!

1. Who is the one-legged pirate in *Treasure Island*?

Long John Gold
Long John Silver
Long John Copper

2. In *Treasure Island*, what is Jim Hawkins' job?

Captain
Cook
Cabin-boy

3. Who is *Peter Pan*'s arch pirate enemy?

Captain Hook
Captain America
Captain Kirk

Fictional Pirates Quiz

4. Which *animal* ate this captain's arm?

Crocodile
Macaw
Tiger

5. Which *cartoon* pirate was created in 1950?

Captain Kegwash
Captain Hogwash
Captain Pugwash

6. Which film stars Geena Davis as a *woman* pirate?

Cutlet Island
Cut Throat Island
Cut-price Island

Parrots & Other Animals

Parrot Jokes

Why didn't Long John Silver have
any aspirins?

Because his parrots-ate-em-all!
(paracetamol).

What's a parrot's favourite food?

Polly-filler!

Who has a parrot sitting on his
shoulder shouting 'Pieces-of-four'?

Short John Silver!

When I was stranded on a desert
island, I ate my parrot.

What did it taste like?

Duck, goose, chicken, turkey – that
parrot could imitate anything!

Sickness And Health

Pirate ships were really unhealthy places. Nearly half the crew might actually die during a long voyage!

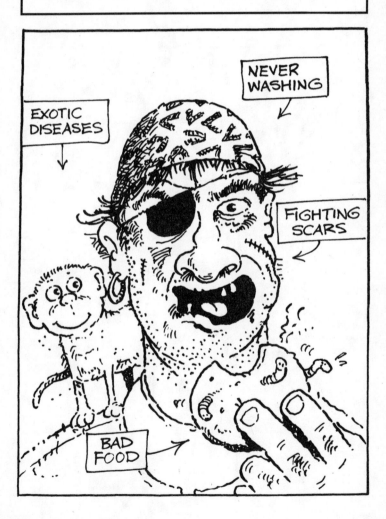

Sickness And Health

Pirates got **yellow fever**, a South American disease from monkeys (via mosquito bites).

or a horrible disease called **dysentery** ...

Scurvy

No fresh fruit or veg meant no Vitamin C.
So pirates got **scurvy** ...

POOR VISION

GUMS BLEED

TEETH FALL OUT

BLOTCHY SKIN

DIARRHOEA

SWOLLEN LEGS

In 1753 they discovered that oranges, lemons and limes helped to prevent scurvy. That's why Americans call British sailors 'limeys'.

Surgery

Pirates had no doctors (unless they captured one), no medicine (unless they stole it) and no anaesthetic (except rum).

Medicine Chest Of Jokes

How do you cure seasickness?

Bolt your food down!

What do you call a pirate floating in the sea?

Bob!

Where do sick pirate ships go?

To the dock!

Today I had diarrhoea, malaria <u>and</u> consumption.

That's terrible!

I know — worst spelling test I can remember!

Putting Ashore

Jake is surprised when *The Leaky Bucket* puts ashore for a week on a deserted island.

SMOKE A PIPE

HUNTING TURTLES AND WILD PIG

FRESH FRUIT

Putting Ashore

COLLECT COCONUTS

FRESH WATER FROM SPRINGS

REPAIR SAILS AND ROPES

Putting Ashore

Every few months the ship is 'careened' – dragged aground for the hull to be cleaned, repaired and made more watertight.

REPLACE WORM-EATEN PLANKS

PAINT HULL WITH TALLOW, BRIMSTONE AND OIL

SCRAPE OFF BARNACLES

REMOVE SEAWEED

TAR

FILL LEAKY BITS WITH ROPE COVERED IN TAR

Putting Ashore

They also put in at 'friendly' ports (like Port Royal in Jamaica) – the only place pirates could actually spend their booty!

Some pirates spent '2 or 3 thousand pieces-of-eight in one night, not leaving themselves a good shirt on their backs'!

Look Out!

The Leaky Bucket is hiding among these islands. On which two spots should Cap'n Blackbird put Bob and Jake, so they can watch **all** the channels in and out of the islands?

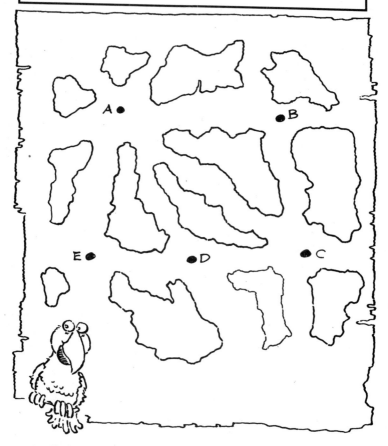

Answer on page 158

GOTCHA!

BLACKBEARD BUMPED OFF IN BATTLE BLOODBATH!

SHOT FIVE TIMES!

Edward Teach, aka the pirate Blackbeard, is dead today – after two years' terrorising the U.S. coasts of Virginia and Carolina.

Lieutenant Maynard of the British Navy despatched the famous villain during a terrible battle. Blackbeard was shot five times and received twenty sword wounds.

His head was cut off and tied to the bowsprit of Maynard's ship!

YOUR HAIR'S ON FIRE!

Bristol-born Blackbeard was a giant man with a twisted nose and a huge beard.

He tied cords soaked in gunpowder into his hair and set fire to the cords so they smouldered!

He also drank rum mixed with gunpowder!

£100 BOUNTY

Blackbeard's bloody end came at his base in Ocracoke Inlet. He was forcing local ships to pay a toll, and sharing the cash with the governor of North Carolina. Locals asked the governor of Virginia for help. The price on Blackbeard's head was £100!

SEA OF BLOOD

Blackbeard, wearing three pairs of pistols and belt full of daggers and cutlasses, was aboard his ship the *Adventure* when Maynard attacked.

The battle was intense. According to one witness, 'the sea was tinctured with blood around the vessel.'

BLACKBEARD SHOT ME!

First mate Israel Hands was once shot through the knee by the villainous pirate.

Raged Hands: 'Blackbeard said if he didn't kill one of his crew now and again, we'd forget who he was!'

IS THERE A DOCTOR IN THE HOUSE?

Blackbeard blockaded the harbour of Charleston, South Carolina. He kidnapped a town elder and his kid and demanded a chest of medicine in return!

14 WIVES!

Blackbeard, who also used the names Drummond and Thatch, had 14 wives!

He once left a wife on a desert island to look after a chest of treasure.

When he came back she had vanished – along with the chest!

IN WHICH BATTLE WAS BLACKBEARD KILLED?
HIS LAST ONE!

Havens

Like all outlaws pirates need a safe place to hide from the law, spend their loot and plan their next raid.

But the most popular haven was **Madagascar ...**

Havens

MADAGASCAR ×××××

5 – SCAR RESORT!

The Pirates' Haven!

If you want gorgeous sunsets, empty beaches, exotic food and a complete lack of law or justice – look no further than the sun-drenched shores of Madagascar.

Located in the Indian Ocean off the coast of East Africa, this beautiful tropical island paradise is ideal for **pirate** activity:

- Only a few km from the **shipping** routes to India and China
- Full of **hidden** creeks, remote beaches and shallow inlets
- Perfect for holing up after a **raid**

Voted a <u>5-scar</u> resort by *Which Pirate?* Madagascar is home to 1,500 villains including James Plantain and Abraham Samuel.

Book early to avoid disappointment!

Sir Henry Morgan

Sir Henry Morgan

Sir Henry Morgan

Sir Henry Morgan

Execution

Captured pirates were beheaded, crucified, hanged or rotted away in foul prison ships.

Execution

The British Admiralty and Hempen
Entertainment proudly present

A PUBLIC HANGING!

Of A Notorious Pirate

A GREAT DAY OUT FOR THE
WHOLE FAMILY!

BRING YOUR OWN ROTTEN VEGETABLES
PRIZE FOR THE BEST INSULT!

Meet at
EXECUTION DOCK, WAPPING
Low tide watermark

---

1 p.m. PRISONER ARRIVES
2 p.m. THE HANGING
3 p.m. DRAG THE BODY THROUGH
THE STREETS

Refreshments available!

Gruesome Facts!

Hanging was called 'Dancing the Hempen Jig'.

Relatives pulled on the prisoner's legs to speed their death.

Before his hanging, pirate Denis McCarthy kicked his silver-buckled shoes into the crowd.

Pirates' bodies might be tarred and hung in cages or 'gibbets' as a warning.

It is said pirates feared being measured for their gibbets more than hanging!

A Gibbet Of Jokes!

What do hangmen read?

Noose papers!

What's the last thing a pirate ever does?

He bites the dust!

What's the definition of a noose?

A real pain in the neck!

Why did the hangman go to hospital?

He was feeling a bit ropey!

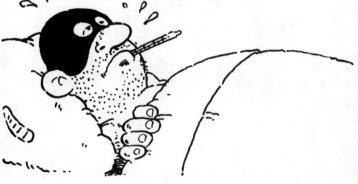

Goodbye

It's the end of Jake's adventure, and he says goodbye to his new pirate friends.

First Prize

The next week at school, Jake wins first prize for his 'Pirate' project!

Treasure Map

The answer to each question is pictured as a symbol on the treasure map. Cross out each answer-symbol until only one is left – the treasure is buried under it!

1. The price on Blackbeard's head.
2. Hard tack.
3. You need a capstan to raise it.
4. They're worth 8 reals.
5. What Black Bart saved from the King Solomon.
6. Madagascar earned 5 of these.
7. Where treasure is kept on board.
8. Sign of the Hempen Jig.
9. A gibbet.
10. Black Bart's favourite drink.
11. Not allowed in the gunpowder magazine.
12. A Bring-'em-near.
13. The ship's 'Cat'.
14. Pays for a pirate's burial.

Treasure Map

DAGGER ISLAND!

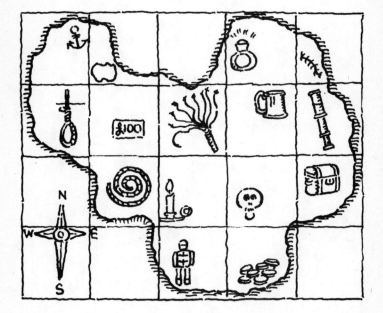

Answer on page 158

Answers

Rigging Maze
page 18

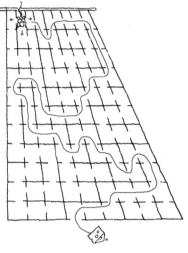

Buccaneer Search
page 28

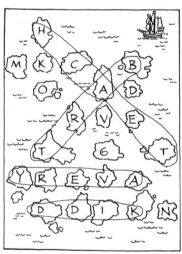

Answers

Mind the Sharks!
page 59

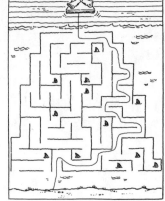

Telescopes
page 117

Fictional Pirates Quiz
pages 125–6

1. Long John Silver
2. Cabin-boy
3. Captain Hook
4. Crocodile
5. Captain Pugwash
6. Cut Throat Island

Answers

Look Out!
page 138

Cap'n Blackbeard put Bob and Jake
at A and C.

Dagger Island
page 155

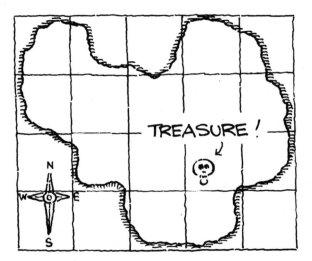

Index